THE 10

Most Outstanding American Women

Deborah Nyman • Ricki Wortzman

Series Editor
Jeffrey D. Wilhelm

Much thought, debate, and research went into choosing and ranking the 10 items in each book in this series. We realize that everyone has his or her own opinion of what is most significant, revolutionary, amazing, deadly, and so on. As you read, you may agree with our choices, or you may be surprised — and that's the way it should be!

an imprint of

■SCHOLASTIC

www.scholastic.com/librarypublishing

A Rubicon book published in association with Scholastic Inc.

Ru'bicon © 2007 Rubicon Publishing Inc.
www.rubiconpublishing.com

Associate Publishers: Kim Koh, Miriam Bardswich
Project Editor: Amy Land
Editor: Bettina Fehrenbach
Creative Director: Jennifer Drew
Senior Designer: Jeanette MacLean
Graphic Designers: Doug Baines, Waseem Bashar, Rebecca Buchanan, Dana Delle Cese-Ahluwalia, Jen Harvey, Kerri Knibb, Brandon Köpke, and Julie Whatman

The publisher gratefully acknowledges the following for permission to reprint copyrighted material in this book.

Every reasonable effort has been made to trace the owners of copyrighted material and to make due acknowledgment. Any errors or omissions drawn to our attention will be gladly rectified in future editions.

"Fable for Tomorrow," an excerpt from *Silent Spring*, by Rachel Carson. Copyright © 1962 by Rachel L. Carson, renewed 1990 by Roger Christie. Reprinted with permission of Houghton Mifflin Company. All rights reserved.

"Oprah Winfrey, Fulfilling Pledge to Mandela, Opens South African School for Girls" (excerpt), by Celean Jacobson. From Associated Press, January 3, 2007. Reprinted with permission.

Library and Archives Canada Cataloguing in Publication

Nyman, Debbie
        The 10 most outstanding American women / Debbie Nyman, Ricki Wortzman.

ISBN 978-1-55448-468-3

        1. Readers (Elementary). 2. Readers—American—Women.
I. Wortzman, Ricki II. Title. III. Title: Ten most outstanding American women.

PE1117.N95268 2007   428.6   C2007-904044-6

2 3 4 5 6 7 8 9 10 11   10   20 19 18 17 16 15 14 13 12 11

Printed in Singapore

Contents

What a Woman!

Have you ever voted for the most outstanding student or athlete in your school? If you did, how did you make your choice?

Countless American women, past and present, can be described as outstanding. Some have broken Olympic records, and others have smashed social barriers. Some have blasted to outer space, and still others have entered fields of work or positions of leadership where no woman has achieved before.

So, how did we select just 10 women for this book? With a lot of difficulty! Through their drive and determination, the women on our list have made personal sacrifices to realize their dreams. They have advocated for the rights of women, children, and minorities and fought for justice in the workplace. Through their actions, they have shaped American history and changed American society for the better. And they have opened doors for other women and created new possibilities for many.

We invite you to step into the shoes of our 10 most outstanding American women. As you read about their achievements, ask yourself:

Who is the most Outstanding American Woman?

10 WENDY KOPP

In 2004, Wendy Kopp received the John F. Kennedy New Frontier Award from Senator Edward Kennedy. The yearly award is given to Americans under the age of 40 whose work in public service is changing their communities and the country.

ROOTS: Born in 1967 in Dallas, Texas

ON THE JOB: Education activist, founder and president of Teach For America

OUTSTANDING ACHIEVEMENT: Wendy Kopp's program enlists talented college graduates to volunteer to teach students in America's needy rural and urban public schools.

> *"It is exhausting to have true passions, but it is hard to imagine anything more fulfilling."*
> — WENDY KOPP

Wendy Kopp believed that all children in the United States should receive an excellent education. Many share this belief, but Kopp did something about it. Her plan was to form a group of bright, young teachers and place them in schools in lower-income districts.

Kopp started out by writing a passionate letter to the president of the United States. The president's office replied with a standard rejection. She then decided to try to start this nonprofit organization by herself. Kopp had to raise $2.5 million in the first year, but she wasn't worried. She later said that her biggest asset was that she just didn't understand what was impossible.

It took a while, but Kopp succeeded in raising the money. Teach For America (TFA) was born. The hard part wasn't over, though. She still had to convince talented graduates to start teaching in some of the nation's toughest schools instead of accepting better-paying jobs. Even though Kopp had neither teaching nor business experience, she was able to put her dream into action.

WENDY KOPP

DARE TO DREAM

Kopp knew that too many children from poor communities were falling behind and dropping out of school. She dreamed of a system that would guarantee these kids an excellent education. As a senior at Princeton University, Kopp planned to have graduates of top colleges teach children in low-income communities.

> **?** Have you ever noticed anything that you think is unfair in your school? What actions could you take to change this situation?

GETTING THERE

Raising $2.5 million in funding wasn't easy, but Kopp did it. She also had to recruit graduates from the country's top universities. Because this was 1990 (before e-mail), Kopp had to hand out a lot of flyers.

Her hard work paid off. Although Ivy League college graduates could easily move into high-paying jobs, many of them wanted to make a positive contribution to the education of children. From there, a movement was born.

Ivy League: *group of schools with an excellent academic reputation*

HER LEGACY

Today, 4,400 TFA members are working in 25 states, and TFA is still growing. By 2010, TFA estimates it will have over 7,000 members in over 30 regions. Since its creation in 1990, about 17,000 young college graduates have participated in TFA. They have helped more than 2.5 million students.

> **?** How does making sure that each and every child has an excellent education change the world?

The Expert Says...

" By recruiting top math and science graduates to teach in underserved communities, Teach For America is helping encourage bright young minds to explore a future in science while building a new generation of leaders in education. "

— Jean L. Lim, president of the Amgen Foundation

In 2006, Teach For America attracted 19,000 applicants. They came from top universities and colleges across the country.

Quick Fact

In a 2005 survey, 75% of school principals believed that Teach For America teachers were more effective than other school teachers. Also, the results of one study showed that the students of TFA teachers had higher math score gains than their peers.

POSSESSED BY AN IDEA

In this excerpt from a speech Wendy Kopp gave in May 2006 at the University of North Carolina, she explained how she came up with the idea for TFA.

"Thinking back to my own senior year in college, I wasn't intending to start something like Teach For America — or to start anything at all for that matter. As a college senior I was ... generally struggling in my search for something that I really wanted to do. My generation was dubbed the 'Me Generation.'

People thought all we wanted to do was focus on ourselves and make a lot of money. But that didn't strike me as right. I felt as if thousands of us talented, driven graduating seniors were searching for a way to make a social impact but simply couldn't find the opportunity to do so.

Well, during my senior fall, I helped organize a conference ... where one of the topics was the shortage of qualified teachers in urban and rural communities. It was at that conference that I thought of an idea: Why doesn't our country have a national teacher corps that recruits us to teach in low-income communities the same way we're being recruited to work on Wall Street?

From that moment, I was possessed by this idea — I thought it would make a huge difference in kids' lives, and that ultimately it could change the very consciousness of our country, by influencing the thinking and career paths of a generation of leaders. ..."

dubbed: *called*

Quick Fact

In December 1994, *TIME* magazine recognized Wendy Kopp as one of the 40 most promising leaders under 40.

Take Note

Kopp didn't have any teaching experience, but she followed her dream and created Teach For America. She overcame obstacles and has had a major impact on society by providing education for needy kids. She stands tall at #10 on our list.
• Kopp said, "My generation was dubbed the 'Me Generation.'" What do you think she means by this? How does Kopp show that she is not a typical member of the "Me Generation"?

MARIA TALL

Maria Tallchief's electrifying performance in Firebird was considered the best of her career. Her choreographer husband had created the ballet just for her.

CHIEF

ROOTS: Born January 24, 1925, in Fairfax, Oklahoma

ON THE JOB: Prima, or star, ballerina

OUTSTANDING ACHIEVEMENT: At a time when it was believed Americans couldn't dance with the best, Maria Tallchief became an international ballet star.

"A ballerina takes steps given to her and makes them her own. Each individual brings something different to the same role."

— MARIA TALLCHIEF

President Eisenhower declared Maria Tallchief Woman of the Year in 1953. Why? Because she conquered the world of ballet! The Europeans had dominated the dance stage for years. So it was a big deal when the international ballet world was wowed for the first time by an American dancer. Oh, and did we mention she's part Native American too?

Maria Tallchief captivated ballet fans in America and Europe. She also won the attention of the famous choreographer George Balanchine, who wrote some of his best works for her, including *Firebird*. They were married in 1946. Together they worked at what is known today as the New York City Ballet.

Tallchief's magic as a ballerina is well described by critic Walter Terry, who wrote of her 1954 performance in Balanchine's *The Nutcracker*: "Maria Tallchief, as the Sugar Plum Fairy, is herself a creature of magic, dancing the seemingly impossible with effortless beauty of movement, electrifying us with her brilliance, enchanting us with her radiance of being."

---

choreographer: *person who designs the steps for a dancer*

MARIA TALLCHIEF

DARE TO DREAM

Maria Tallchief grew up on the Osage reservation in Oklahoma. Her mother was of European descent and her father was Native American. She loved to sing, play the piano, and dance. When she was three years old, she attended a ballet class. She began to dream of becoming a ballerina. When she was eight, the family moved to Los Angeles so that she could get proper training in ballet.

Quick Fact

Maria Tallchief's original name was Elizabeth Marie Tall Chief. In high school she changed her last name to Tallchief, still preserving her heritage.

GETTING THERE

In Los Angeles, Tallchief studied ballet with a noted Russian teacher and choreographer. At 17, Tallchief left Los Angeles to continue her studies in New York City. She then joined the Ballet Russe de Monte Carlo and quickly began performing solo dances.

Tallchief was the first Native American to dance and be accepted by audiences around the world. However, her fame and talent did not totally shield her from discrimination because of her Native American heritage.

? Maria Tallchief sometimes faced name-calling by audiences because of her Native American background. How would you handle this if you were in her situation?

HER LEGACY

Tallchief founded the Chicago City Ballet in 1980 and served as the artistic director through 1987. There she directed and trained countless young dancers. Her pride in her heritage inspired Native Americans to pursue their dreams in whatever field they chose.

Maria Tallchief puts on a ceremonial headdress during a hometown celebration in 1953.

The Expert Says...

"She was — is — deeply American and deeply proud of her Osage background. She was a 'ballerina' in the classic sense — grand, glamorous, authoritative: a diva."

— Robert Gottlieb, *The New York Times*

10   **9**   8   7   6

Make My Day

On February 27, 1998, the mayor of Chicago, Richard M. Daley, declared March 12 a day to honor Maria Tallchief. This **proclamation** explains why she deserves this honor.

Proclamation

WHEREAS, Maria Tallchief is recognized throughout the world as one of the first and greatest American-trained ballet dancers of international importance; and

WHEREAS, Maria Tallchief is one of the greatest Native American dancers of all times, the daughter of an Osage Indian born in Fairfax, Oklahoma; and

WHEREAS, Maria Tallchief founded the Chicago City Ballet in 1980 and served as its director until 1987; and

WHEREAS, Maria Tallchief was one of Robert Joffrey's most revered ballerinas, a source of ongoing inspiration and a tribute to the American Art of Dance; and

WHEREAS, Maria Tallchief created roles in many ballets, including Balanchine's *Firebird*, *Orpheus*, and *Scotch Symphony*; and ...

NOW, THEREFORE, I, RICHARD M. DALEY, MAYOR OF THE CITY OF CHICAGO, do hereby proclaim March 12, 1998, to be Maria Tallchief Day in Chicago, in recognition of all her contributions to the world of dance and to the cultural life of the city of Chicago.

Richard M. Daley
Mayor
Dated this 27th day of February, 1998

WHEREAS: *formal way of saying "since"*

Quick Fact

After Tallchief's amazing performance in *Firebird*, one audience member said, "The cheering was so loud it was as if we were in a football stadium instead of a theater. I thought the roof would cave in."

Take Note

Maria Tallchief glides into #9 because she broke social barriers by being the first Native American to be a prima ballerina, opening the door for other minority groups in this field.

• Tallchief was awarded the National Medal of Arts for her work as a mentor. If you could choose a mentor for yourself, who would you choose? How could a mentor help you to achieve your goals?

5   4   3   2   1

At the 1956 Olympics in Australia, Rudolph won a bronze medal when she was only 16 years old.

LPH

ROOTS: Born June 23, 1940, in St. Bethlehem, Tennessee; died November 12, 1994, in Brentwood, Tennessee

ON THE JOB: Olympic athlete

OUTSTANDING ACHIEVEMENT: Rudolph was the first American woman to win three Olympic gold medals.

"But when you come from a large, wonderful family, there's always a way to achieve your goals."

— WILMA RUDOLPH

Imagine being told as a child that you will never walk again. Then imagine winning not just one, but three, Olympic gold medals! Impossible? Not if you're Wilma Rudolph.

Rudolph faced many challenges, such as illness and discrimination. As a young child, she suffered from polio. Her doctors told her she would walk only with the help of braces. But Rudolph and her family did not give up. They worked hard to overcome this obstacle.

As an African American, it was difficult to get medical treatment in Tennessee in those days. Rudolph had to travel 50 miles to see a doctor who would treat African Americans. She did this twice a week, for two years. With treatment and exercise, she was able to walk normally at the age of 12. Just four years later, she won her first Olympic medal!

polio: *disease (now rare) that causes muscle weakness and can lead to paralysis*

WILMA RUDOLPH

DARE TO DREAM

Rudolph did not even weigh five pounds at birth. After polio left her leg deformed and weakened, Rudolph dreamed of walking without a brace. Every day her siblings massaged her leg and made sure that she kept her braces on. By the age of 12, she was able to walk normally again. Upon conquering her first dream of walking, Rudolph then dreamed of being an athlete.

? Rudolph was determined to walk without braces. Think of a challenge or obstacle that you have faced in your life. How did you overcome it?

GETTING THERE

Once she was fit again, Rudolph devoted herself to sports. She joined the school basketball team. It was three years before her coach allowed her to play in a game. Once Rudolph got the chance to play, she became an instant star. The coach of Tennessee State University saw her talent and invited her to join the track team. She trained hard to build stamina and speed. By age 16, Rudolph was running for the Olympics and won a bronze medal!

HER LEGACY

Rudolph grew up in Tennessee, which was racially divided at the time. She dreamed that someday African Americans would have the same rights as white Americans, especially in health care and education. In 1960, when she returned to her hometown with three gold medals from the Rome Olympics, she persuaded the governor of Tennessee to allow her parade and celebration to be an integrated event, meaning that both blacks and whites would attend together.

Rudolph continues to be an inspiration for athletes. She created the Wilma Rudolph Foundation, a nonprofit, amateur sports program, which provides free coaching in a variety of sports.

Rudolph said that she was as proud of the integrated homecoming celebration as she was of her gold medals.

The Expert Says...

" [Wilma Rudolph] did more than promote her country. In her soft-spoken, gracious manner, she paved the way for African American athletes, both men and women, who came later. "

— M.B. Roberts, ESPN.com

STAMP OF APPROVAL

NEWS RELEASE:

To honor Wilma Rudolph's achievements, the U.S. Postal Service decided to put Wilma's picture on a U.S. postage stamp.

June 22, 2004

WASHINGTON — Wilma Rudolph will receive one of the nation's highest tributes when the U.S. Postal Service issues a postage stamp in her honor during a special press conference and ceremony July 14 in Sacramento, CA. Rudolph's extraordinary athletic talents inspired generations of female athletes and the physically disabled.

"We are delighted to honor Wilma Rudolph's accomplishments, both on and beyond the track, as part of our Distinguished Americans stamp series," said Henry A. Pankey, Vice President, Emergency Preparedness, U.S. Postal Service, who will dedicate the stamp. "Wilma Rudolph was simply amazing. She overcame a number of debilitating illnesses to become one of this nation's greatest athletes. She taught us, among other things, not to allow our circumstances to hinder our potential to succeed." ...

Rudolph retired from running in 1962 at the height of her success. She worked as a teacher and a coach, and in the early 1980s established the Wilma Rudolph Foundation. ...

debilitating: *devastating; weakening*
hinder: *hold back*

If you could select someone to be recognized with a stamp, whom would you choose? Why?

Quick Fact

European fans loved Wilma Rudolph. They called her "The Black Gazelle" and "The Black Pearl." A fan even stole her shoes in Berlin!

Take Note

Like Maria Tallchief, Wilma Rudolph faced racial discrimination. She is ranked #8 because she had to overcome incredible physical challenges to achieve her goals.

- Wilma Rudolph used her celebrity status to try to break down racial barriers. Think of other celebrities who have used their status to break down racial or social barriers. How did they do it?

Sally Ride retired from NASA in 1987. She was inducted into the U.S. Astronaut Hall of Fame at Kennedy Space Center on June 21, 2003.

ROOTS: Born May 26, 1951, in Los Angeles, California

ON THE JOB: Astronaut

OUTSTANDING ACHIEVEMENT: Ride was the first American woman to fly in space.

"Our future lies with today's kids and tomorrow's space exploration."

— SALLY RIDE

What does it take to become an astronaut? Sally Ride had the "right stuff" and stood out among 8,000 other applicants! Up until the 1970s, NASA (National Aeronautics and Space Administration) had accepted and trained only male military test pilots for the space program. This time they were searching for people who could perform complex experiments in space. Sally Ride's outstanding skills as a scientist got her the job.

She trained tirelessly as a mission specialist. When she blasted off in the *Challenger* in 1983, Ride became the first American woman in space. On that flight, the five-person crew sent out two communications satellites. They were the first to use a robot arm to release and retrieve a satellite in space. In 1984, Ride made a second space flight, also on board the *Challenger*. In total, she spent more than 343 hours in space.

Ride was in Florida training for a third flight when the *Challenger* exploded just after liftoff. She was appointed to the investigating team to find out what went wrong. Her reports helped explain the technical difficulties and gave direction for the future of space travel.

Now a retired astronaut, Ride works to ensure that girls see that they too can have fun — and excel — when they study math and science. She inspires, motivates, and encourages girls to learn so that they can discover new worlds.

SALLY RIDE

DARE TO DREAM

Ride, a natural athlete, dreamed of being a professional tennis player. When she realized she wasn't good enough, she decided to return to her studies. She obtained degrees in English, physics, and astrophysics (a study of how physics relates to astronomy). She had never dreamed of becoming an astronaut, but Ride was one of only six women chosen by NASA for training. She now encourages kids to "dream big and work hard."

GETTING THERE

In 1978, Ride joined NASA when they accepted women for the astronaut class for the first time. The training was very challenging and included parachute jumping, water survival, zero-gravity (weightlessness) training, radio communications, and navigation.

Sally Ride, third from right, was one of six women selected for the astronaut class of 1978. Among the women selected were a biochemist, an electrical engineer, a geologist, a physicist, and a surgeon.

Quick Fact

Improving science education for children is important to Sally Ride. She has written several science books for children: *To Space and Back*, *Voyager*, *The Third Planet*, *The Mystery of Mars*, and *Exploring Our Solar System*.

HER LEGACY

Sally Ride is concerned about how few women there are in math, science, and engineering programs. She has helped establish educational programs, camps, and science festivals to encourage girls to study the sciences. Her mission is to help girls believe that through creativity, imagination, and dedication, they can reach for the stars and achieve their dreams.

? Studies show that by high school, twice as many boys as girls enroll in science and math. How can this be changed?

Ride monitors control panels from the pilot's chair on the flight deck.

The Expert Says...

"Sally Ride is smart in a very special way. ... Sally can get everything she knows together and bring it to ... where you need it.

— George Abbey, NASA's director of flight crew operations

Ride, Sally Ride!

The above headline appeared in June 1983. Check out the list below for some of the challenges that Ride had to face as the first American woman in space, which was still dominated by men at the time.

• Before her first flight, Ride took part in a press conference with the rest of the *Challenger* crew. A male reporter asked if she wept when things went wrong. This question still angers Ride when she thinks about it.

 What does this question tell you about the reporter's beliefs?

• NASA even supplied makeup on the flight, but Ride did not use it.

• Ride was all over the news because she was the first American woman in space. Ride says that she never wanted the attention. "My personality was the personality of a physicist who wanted to be an astronaut," Ride said. "Not the personality of someone who wanted to be a public figure."

Quick Fact

Of the hundreds of astronauts who have traveled to space, only 40 were women. Sally Ride paved the way for Mae Jemison who, in 1992, was the first female African American in space. A year later, Ellen Ochoa was the first Hispanic-American astronaut.

Take Note

Sally Ride ranks #7 for being the first American woman to fly into space and for the work she is doing to encourage young women to continue studying math and science.
• Some jobs are still held mostly by men and some held mostly by women. Why is this?

5   4   3   2   1

Maya Angelou is fluent in six languages: English, French, Spanish, Italian, Arabic, and West African Fanti.

ROOTS: Born April 4, 1928, in St. Louis, Missouri

ON THE JOB: Poet, writer, historian, educator, director, actor, producer, and civil rights activist

OUTSTANDING ACHIEVEMENT: Maya Angelou is best known as a great voice of our time and for her book *I Know Why the Caged Bird Sings*.

"Courage is the most important of all the virtues, because without courage you can't practice any other virtue consistently."

— MAYA ANGELOU

Maya Angelou is a woman of many talents. She has written books and poetry, has acted in and produced movies and musicals, and has even released an album as a singer! Her books and poetry have opened America's eyes to racial discrimination, suffering, and poverty. She wrote the poem "On the Pulse of Morning" and read it at the inauguration of President Bill Clinton in 1993. This was only the second time that a poem was read during a presidential inauguration.

Angelou is also a civil rights activist. She worked closely with civil rights leaders Malcolm X and Dr. Martin Luther King. The deaths of these two men devastated Angelou, but she continues to inspire through her words.

Universities have honored Angelou for her lectures and speeches. In both 1993 and 2002, Angelou received the Grammy Award for Best Spoken Word Album. In 2005, Angelou was one of 25 inspirational women honored by Oprah Winfrey, the #2 most outstanding woman on our list.

Maya Angelou continues to inspire through her words.

MAYA ANGELOU

DARE TO DREAM

Angelou dreamed of how easy her life would be if she were a white girl with blonde hair. Her own life was not easy. At the age of seven, she was violently attacked by her mother's boyfriend. As a result of this trauma, she refused to speak for five years. Angelou found her voice again when she started to write.

Quick Fact

Angelou's first book, *I Know Why the Caged Bird Sings*, was published in 1970 and was on *The New York Times* best-seller list for two years. It was inspired by her childhood and explains her decision to remain silent as a child.

GETTING THERE

Angelou's parents divorced when she was only three. She grew up living with her grandmother. By the age of 16, she was a single mother supporting her son. In her early 20s, Angelou was singing and performing on stage. In the late 1950s, she moved to New York City where she became involved with young black writers and activists.

For over 10 years in the 1960s, Angelou lived in Africa. Her work as a writer and editor for several newspapers in Africa gave her a sense of connection to her past. After her book *I Know Why the Caged Bird Sings* was published, Angelou became a national figure. She was sought after to teach, lecture, and write.

? Maya Angelou once said, "If you don't like something, change it. If you can't change it, change your attitude. Don't complain." When have you tried to change something you didn't like? What was the outcome?

HER LEGACY

Angelou inspired and captivated millions when she read her poem at the inauguration of President Bill Clinton in 1993. She is a gifted writer and speaker, but Angelou is first and foremost a teacher. She believes that "peace and justice should belong to every person, everywhere, all the time." She continues to inspire many to achieve their dreams. She devotes much of her time to improving conditions for women in developing nations, mainly in Africa. Angelou wants to create a better life for women who are poor, abused, and single mothers.

Angelou has published more than 20 books, all of which are still in print.

The Expert Says...

" We have all heard about the power of a picture to speak a thousand words. What we've gotten through Dr. Angelou is the power of a single word to affect us with a thousand emotions. "

— Loretha Jones, film director and producer

Words of Wisdom

You probably won't get a chance to hang out with Maya Angelou and discuss the meaning of life. Luckily, you can "hear" her voice in these quotes. As Oprah Winfrey says, Maya Angelou "speaks of what she knows."

"Being a woman is hard work."

"We may encounter many defeats but we must not be defeated."

"Words mean more than what is set down on paper. It takes the human voice to infuse them with deeper meaning."

"... Talk, use the language, men. Use the language, women. That is the only thing which really separates us from the rats and the rhinoceros. It is the ability to say how we feel. 'I believe this.' 'I need this.' Start to talk, please."

"How important it is for us to recognize and celebrate our heroes and she-roes!"

Maya Angelou reads a poem at the inauguration of President Bill Clinton.

"I believe that every person is born with talent."

"Music was my refuge. I could crawl into the space between the notes and curl my back to loneliness."

Take Note

Maya Angelou is #6 because her words and her work in civil rights and social justice have helped shape America. She overcame challenges and has contributed to education, politics, literature, and the arts. She is in her 80s and is still going strong!
• How do you think people's lives are enriched through the arts?

2   1

Steinem was inducted into the National Women's Hall of Fame in 1993.

ROOTS: Born March 25, 1934, in Toledo, Ohio

ON THE JOB: Journalist, author, feminist leader, and women's rights advocate

OUTSTANDING ACHIEVEMENT: Gloria Steinem has been an activist all of her life. She is best known as an outspoken leader in the fight for women's rights.

"We've begun to raise daughters more like sons ... but few have the courage to raise our sons more like our daughters."

— GLORIA STEINEM

Do you believe women and men have equal rights today? Do you think women should still be fighting for equal rights? Gloria Steinem has been fighting for women's rights for decades, and she believes women still have a long way to go.

As a young investigative journalist in New York City in the early 1960s, Steinem expressed her passion for social justice and equality. She wrote articles on civil and women's rights. She also wrote about the antiwar movement during the Vietnam War. With the support of other feminists, she dedicated herself to bringing women's issues into politics.

In 1972, Steinem founded *Ms.*, a feminist magazine that helped speed up the women's movement. She continues to keep women's issues at the forefront with her articles and speeches. Now in her seventies, Steinem is still an icon of the women's movement.

 Do you agree with what Gloria Steinem says in her quotation? Why or why not? What qualities do you think are important in raising children today?

GLORIA STEINEM—AMANDA EDWARDS/GETTY IMAGES

GLORIA STEINEM

DARE TO DREAM

Steinem was the daughter of a journalist and the granddaughter of a suffragette. After graduating from Smith College, she studied in India for two years. Aware of the poverty and injustice in the world, Steinem dreamed of becoming a journalist — so that she could tell important stories about social justice and hopefully change the world.

suffragette: *woman who campaigns for a woman's right to vote*

? Do you feel that women and men are 100% equal in every area? Why or why not? If not, what else could be done to achieve equality?

GETTING THERE

Steinem did not have an easy life growing up. After her parents divorced when she was eight, she and her mother were forced to live in poverty. To make matters worse, her mother fell into a deep depression, and Steinem had to care for her.

Pursuing a journalism career was no piece of cake for women in the 1960s. In those days, males were typically hired over females. In response to this sexism, Steinem wrote articles for magazines exposing social injustices. She organized women to speak out and demand equal jobs and pay in the workforce. In 1972, Steinem, as part of the Women's Action Alliance, gained funding for the first mass circulation feminist magazine, *Ms.* She was its editor for 15 years.

Gloria Steinem chats with the marchers in midtown Manhattan prior to the start of the International Women's Day March in 1975.

HER LEGACY

Steinem continues to write and lecture. Much has changed for women since she began speaking out, including progress in the workforce. Through the Women's Media Center, a Web site Steinem helped found in 2004, her words continue to inspire women everywhere.

The Expert Says...

" So now Gloria has touched all of our lives; both of my daughters' and mine. My daughters and the daughters of countless other boomers will build on the legacy that Gloria Steinem represents. "

— Nancy Mills, former Emmy Award-winning NBC correspondent

Quick Fact

The Equal Rights Amendment (ERA) was written in 1923 and was proposed to Congress every year for five decades. It was finally passed in 1972 and sent to the states to pass. Not enough states have passed it to become an official amendment to the Constitution. Steinem has fought for years to have this amendment passed.

A Lifetime of Achievements

Since the 1950s, Gloria Steinem has accomplished so much. From journalism to writing to civil rights, this activist has a lot to be proud of! Check out her achievements in the fact cards below.

Contributing editor to *New York* magazine

Year: 1968
Achievement: Steinem joined the founding staff of *New York* magazine and started her own political column, "The City Politic."

National Women's Political Caucus

Year: 1971
Achievement: Steinem joined other female activists in forming the National Women's Political Caucus. This was created to encourage women to vote in the 1972 presidential election.

caucus: *committee*

Writer and publisher

Years: 1983, 1986, 1992, 1994, and 2006
Achievement: Steinem wrote and published many books including *Outrageous Acts and Everyday Rebellion*, *Marilyn: Norma Jean*, *Revolution from Within: A Book of Self-Esteem*, *Moving Beyond Words*, and *Doing Sixty and Seventy*.

Gloria Steinem marches at the Women's Rights rally October 7, 1995 in New York City.

National Conference of Women

Year: 1977
Achievement: Steinem participated in this conference in Houston, Texas. It was the first of its kind where women gathered together to measure the progress that they had made and identify barriers to equality.

Take Note

Like many of the other women you have read about in this book, Gloria Steinem spoke out for women at a time when many others didn't. For her contribution to the women's movement in America, she is ranked #5 on our list, ahead of Maya Angelou.
• In order to have achieved what she did, what personality characteristics do you think Steinem has?

Rachel Carson was named by *TIME* magazine *as one of the most influential people in the 20th century.*

SON

ROOTS: Born May 27, 1907, in Springdale, Pennsylvania; died April 14, 1964, in Silver Spring, Maryland

ON THE JOB: Biologist, writer, and ecologist

OUTSTANDING ACHIEVEMENT: Rachel Carson was bravely speaking out about the environment long before it was cool. She wrote the first book about "thinking green" — and it made a lot of people see red.

"One way to open your eyes is to ask yourself, 'What if I had never seen this before? What if I knew I would never see it again?'"

— RACHEL CARSON

Rachel Carson has been called the "founder of the environmental movement."

Her book *Silent Spring*, published in 1962, is credited with first opening the eyes of the public to the dangers of chemical pesticides. Carson called for a change in attitudes before too much damage was done to the environment. Worried about profits, the chemical industry accused her of being an alarmist. The National Agricultural Chemicals Association spent more than $250,000 to attack Carson's book and her reputation as a scientist. This would be about $1.5 million today.

Carson did not give up. She bravely spoke out, calling on the government to protect the health of the people and the environment.

Rachel Carson died in 1964 of cancer. However, her work continues to inspire people to "think green." In 1992, *Silent Spring* was voted the most influential book of the past 50 years.

RACHEL CARSON

DARE TO DREAM

Rachel Carson was raised by a mother who taught her to love and appreciate nature. Carson was educated as a scientist, and had a great talent for writing. She combined her two loves, writing and nature, and wrote several books about the environment. Through research, she discovered that pesticides were harming the Earth. Fish were turning up dead in lakes and rivers, and birds were dying from eating pesticide-covered plants. Her dream was to help people understand the need to protect the environment.

? Carson used her talent for writing to convince people to take responsibility for the natural world. What do you think is your responsibility to the environment?

GETTING THERE

Rachel Carson began to research the effects of chemicals on the environment after she received a letter from a friend saying that many birds in Cape Cod died after pesticides to control mosquitoes were sprayed from a plane. After thorough research, Carson decided to act and did what she did best — she wrote *Silent Spring*, to warn the public about what lay ahead if pesticide use continued.

? *Silent Spring* is a warning to the world. What other ways can we warn people of environmental concerns?

These fish died because of pesticide use.

HER LEGACY

President John F. Kennedy's Science Advisory Committee confirmed Carson's evidence about the dangers of pesticides and the poisoning of the Earth. Today, former U.S. Vice President Al Gore credits Carson's work for raising awareness about dangers to the environment. Cars are being made to use less gasoline and emit less carbon dioxide. Countries are creating laws to limit factories' release of carbon dioxide. Little by little, the world is reacting the way Carson had hoped.

Quick Fact

At the age of 10, Carson published three stories in a children's magazine and won cash prizes. This success led Carson to think about being a writer.

The Expert Says…

"Yet one shudders to imagine how much more impoverished our habitat would be had *Silent Spring* not sounded the alarm. Well crafted, fearless and succinct, it remains her most celebrated book. …"

— Peter Matthiessen, *TIME* magazine

succinct: *to the point; brief*

Fable for Tomorrow

Book excerpt from _Silent Spring_
By Rachel Carson

There was once a town in the heart of America where all life seemed to live in harmony with its surroundings. The town lay in the midst of a checkerboard of prosperous farms, with fields of grain and hillsides of orchards where, in spring, white clouds of bloom drifted above the green fields. …

Then a strange blight crept over the area and everything began to change. Some evil spell had settled on the community: mysterious maladies swept the flocks of chickens; the cattle and sheep sickened and died. Everywhere was a shadow of death. The farmers spoke of much illness among their families. …

There was a strange stillness. The birds, for example — where had they gone? Many people spoke of them, puzzled and disturbed. The feeding stations in the backyards were deserted. The few birds seen anywhere were moribund; they trembled violently and could not fly. It was a spring without voices. …

This town does not actually exist, but it might easily have a thousand counterparts in America or elsewhere in the world. I know of no community that has experienced all the misfortunes I describe. Yet every one of these disasters has actually happened somewhere, and many real communities have already suffered a substantial number of them. A grim specter has crept upon us almost unnoticed, and this imagined tragedy may easily become a stark reality we all shall know.

blight: _disease_
maladies: _illnesses_
moribund: _dying_
specter: _ghost_

When Carson's work was first published, members of pesticide companies wanted to sue her. They tried to find errors in her research and called her a "hysterical woman."

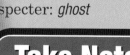 Take Note

Rachel Carson's work has influenced every one of us on this planet. She was one of the first to warn the world of the dangers of polluting the environment. Like the other women in this book, Carson used her voice to educate people. Today, we still hear Rachel Carson's voice through her writing. She is #4 on our list.
- Many of the women on our list have spoken out about and written on what they feel strongly about. Which do you think is more powerful: speaking or writing? Defend your choice.

5   4   3   2   1

NATURE PICTURES/NATURAL EXP—SHUTTERS LOCK; RACHEL CARSON READING—HAL PREY/LESENS/ACUI/TIME; LIFE PICTURES/GETTY IMAGES; DEAD FISH—U.S. FISH AND WILDLIFE SERVICE

Huerta is passionate, determined, outspoken, and fearless.

ERTA

ROOTS: Born April 10, 1930, in Dawson, New Mexico

ON THE JOB: Cofounder of the United Farm Workers, labor leader and organizer, and social activist

OUTSTANDING ACHIEVEMENT: Dolores Huerta stood up for the rights of farmworkers when no one else would. She is considered one of the most powerful and respected leaders of the labor movement.

"I think we showed the world that nonviolence can work to make social change."

— DOLORES HUERTA

Imagine working in the hot sun all day long picking grapes and receiving 25 cents for each bushel picked. Then imagine sleeping in your car because you can't afford to rent a room or buy a house. This was a normal day for farm and immigrant workers in the mid-1900s. Knowing this, Dolores Huerta was determined to make life better for migrant workers.

Along with Cesar Chavez, Huerta formed the United Farm Workers, an organization to protect the rights of workers. She became the face of labor rights. Wherever there were strikes, pickets, or negotiations, Huerta was there. She only used peaceful strategies. She did not believe in using violence to get the job done.

Because of Huerta, many farm and migrant workers now belong to unions, have rights, and are treated fairly. She has touched the lives of immigrants, women, and children who had previously been forgotten in the workforce.

DOLORES HUERTA

DARE TO DREAM

Huerta, who is Mexican American, saw how her father struggled as a farmworker. As a teacher, she was deeply saddened by the poverty of her students, whose parents were farmworkers. She decided to become active in labor unions and began seeking rights for farmworkers.

Quick Fact

Robert F. Kennedy was a strong supporter of Huerta and acknowledged her, the farmworkers, and Chavez's help in winning the 1968 California Democratic Presidential Primary moments before he was assassinated in Los Angeles.

GETTING THERE

In the late 1950s, Huerta began working for the Community Service Organization. She helped register people to vote. She also organized classes for immigrants coming into the U.S. She then joined the Agricultural Workers Association, where she met Cesar Chavez. Together, they worked tirelessly and formed the United Farm Workers in 1962. Working for the union was not an easy task. Huerta was arrested more than 20 times. She was once severely hurt by police during a peaceful protest.

Huerta believed in the power of boycotts and strikes. How effective do you think boycotts can be? Explain your answer.

HER LEGACY

Huerta has been active in many organizations such as the United Farm Workers, the Coalition of Labor Union Women, and the Fund for the Feminist Majority. After 40 years, Huerta continues to work at creating safer and fairer working conditions for farmworkers and immigrant workers.

Quick Fact

In 1998, Huerta received the Eleanor D. Roosevelt Human Rights Award from President Bill Clinton. She was named Woman of the Year in *Ms.* magazine (the magazine that Gloria Steinem began), and she was one of *Ladies' Home Journal*'s 100 Most Important Women of the 20th Century.

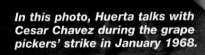

In this photo, Huerta talks with Cesar Chavez during the grape pickers' strike in January 1968.

The Expert Says...

" Dolores Huerta is totally fearless, both mentally and physically. "

— Cesar Chavez, co-founder of the United Farm Workers

Three Reasons Why Dolores Huerta Is #3

Dolores Huerta is known for fighting for civil rights in the workforce. Her work has helped create organizations, which you can read about in the list below.

1 United Farm Workers of America

With the help of Cesar Chavez, Huerta cofounded this organization in 1962 to create better working conditions for farmworkers. The UFW still exists today, and its goals consist of better hours, better wages, and better treatment of farmworkers.

? Choose one of these organizations and learn more about it. How does this organization help minorities or those struggling to make a living?

2 Dolores Huerta Foundation

This nonprofit organization helps to create leadership that will address fair and equal access to health care, housing, education, jobs, and economic resources for underprivileged communities. It also focuses on creating fair conditions for women and youth.

3 Dolores Huerta Learning Academy

This school was founded in 1999 in the most densely populated part of California: Oakland. More than 92 percent of the school's students are Latino and learning English as their second language. The Academy devotes its time to improving the education of its students. Dolores Huerta Learning Academy is committed to providing minority students with the education they need to get ahead.

Take Note

Like Gloria Steinem, Dolores Huerta fought for equal rights. Her quest for social justice and equality for all led her to work alongside men and women standing up for civil rights and the environment. For these reasons Huerta ranks #3.

- Huerta was willing to go to jail for what she believed in. What would be so important to you that you would be willing to take such a strong stand? How would you convince others to join you?

Since The Oprah Winfrey Show *debuted in 1986, it has been the #1 daytime talk show in the United States.*

ROOTS: Born January 29, 1954, in Kosciusko, Mississippi

ON THE JOB: Entertainment executive and businessperson

OUTSTANDING ACHIEVEMENT: Oprah's multimedia empire has made her one of the most influential women in the world. Her kindness and generosity have inspired millions to follow her lead and make the world a better place.

"The opportunity to have a voice and speak to the world every day is a gift."

— OPRAH WINFREY

Oprah Winfrey needs little introduction. She is an international figure known for her TV show, magazine, radio station, book club, acting, and philanthropy.

Each week in the United States, over 48 million viewers watch *The Oprah Winfrey Show*. Winfrey has become America's friend, crying when her guests cry and laughing when they laugh. She tells the truth about herself and shares her views, as if in conversation with her friends. In this way, she empowers her guests, encouraging them to share their opinions. She started a monthly magazine in 2000 called *O, The Oprah Magazine*. It has become one of today's leading women's magazines. In addition, Oprah's Angel Network donates money to those in need and inspires people to make a difference in the lives of others. A $100,000 "Use Your Life Award" is given to people who positively affect others.

It is not hard to see why *TIME* magazine in 2006 named Oprah Winfrey one of the 100 Most Influential People in the World.

philanthropy: *charity; generosity*

DARE TO DREAM

Winfrey was an abused child who was raised in poverty. She credits her grandmother with inspiring her to dream of a better life. Her grandmother taught her to read and recite the Bible at the age of three. Her father also encouraged her to read. This love of books influenced her to instill a love of reading and education in everyone. She believes that education got her where she is today.

 Winfrey believes that books can change lives. Think of the books you have read. What is one book that you think has changed your life in some way? How has it done so?

GETTING THERE

At 17, Winfrey went to work at a radio station in Nashville, Tennessee. By the time she was 19, she was the first African American and youngest person to anchor the news for a TV station. In 1984, she moved to Chicago where she began her popular daytime talk show, *The Oprah Winfrey Show*. In 1986, *The Oprah Winfrey Show* entered national syndication and has become the highest-rated talk show in television history.

HER LEGACY

Winfrey's childhood memories are a driving force behind many of her actions. Using her fame, she started a campaign to create a national database of convicted child abusers. In 1993, President Clinton signed the "Oprah Bill" establishing such a database. Her charity, The Oprah Winfrey Foundation, awards millions of dollars to organizations that support the education of women, children, and families in the U.S. and around the world.

Quick Fact

Oprah's Book Club, started in 1996, is the largest in the world with over 900,000 members. Books that Winfrey selects for her book club skyrocket to the best-seller list in just a few weeks.

The Expert Says...

" … Oprah Winfrey certainly has power. But most important, she has purpose — an abiding commitment to the principles of goodness and generosity that transcend any one individual. "

— Condoleezza Rice, U.S. Secretary of State

transcend: *rise above*

Oprah Winfrey, Fulfilling Pledge to Mandela, Opens South African School for Girls

An article from *Associated Press*
By Celean Jacobson, January 3, 2007

JOHANNESBURG — Talk show host Oprah Winfrey opened a school Tuesday for disadvantaged girls, fulfilling a promise she made to former president Nelson Mandela six years ago.

"I wanted to give this opportunity to girls who had a light so bright that not even poverty could dim that light," Winfrey said at a news conference. Initially, 152 girls will attend the $40 million Oprah Winfrey Leadership Academy for Girls. ...

The project that created a 28-building campus with computer and science laboratories, a library, a theater, and a wellness center began with a $10 million donation from Winfrey in 2002. ...

Winfrey referred repeatedly to her own impoverished childhood and said she was grateful that she at least had a good education, declaring this to be "the most vital aspect of my life."

The idea for the school was born in 2000 at a meeting between Winfrey and Mandela. She said she decided to build the academy in South Africa rather than the United States out of love and respect for Mandela and because of her own African roots.

Winfrey's academy received 3,500 applications from across the country. A total of 152 girls ages 11 and 12 were accepted. To qualify, they had to show both academic and

leadership potential and have a household income of no more than $787 a month. Plans call for the academy eventually to accommodate 450 girls.

Lesego Tlhabanyane, 13, proudly wore her new green and white uniform at the ceremony to raise the South African flag. "I would have had a completely different life if this hadn't happened to me. Now I get a life where I get to be treated like a movie star," she said.

---

impoverished: *poor*
vital: *important*
accommodate: *house*

Take Note

Oprah Winfrey has changed the lives of people in America and around the world. We rank her #2 because she uses her celebrity status to inspire people to act, speak out, and make a difference.
• Choose a cause that you think needs support. How would you convince a celebrity to get involved?

*Eleanor Roosevelt remains an
inspiration to leaders in both civil
rights and women's movements.*

OSEVELT

ROOTS: Born October 11, 1884, in New York City; died November 7, 1962, in New York City

ON THE JOB: Activist, journalist, diplomat, and First Lady

OUTSTANDING ACHIEVEMENT: Eleanor Roosevelt was chair of the committee that was responsible for the drafting of the Declaration of Human Rights. This important document had an effect on human rights world wide.

> *"No one can make you feel inferior without your consent."*
>
> — ELEANOR ROOSEVELT

Eleanor Roosevelt is probably best known for being the First Lady and wife to Franklin Delano Roosevelt, the 32nd president of the United States. However, she was a star in her own right.

Roosevelt was an advocate for the rights of minorities and the poor. She fought to make child labor illegal, establish the minimum wage, and protect workers' rights. She was the force behind the president, who signed executive orders to ban discrimination in the country. As part of the United Nations' Commission on Human Rights, Roosevelt helped to establish the Universal Declaration of Human Rights, which states that "All human beings are born free and equal in dignity and rights."

She was a shy woman with a big heart. Throughout her life, she worked at improving the welfare of human beings. She traveled all over the country, visiting relief projects and surveying working and living conditions among the poor. Her humanitarian efforts have won her respect and love around the world, more than four decades after her death.

Eleanor Roosevelt is our choice of the most outstanding American woman. Turn the page to find out why she is #1.

ELEANOR ROOSEVELT

Eleanor Roosevelt
USA 20¢

DARE TO DREAM

Eleanor Roosevelt came from a well-to-do family. She disapproved of how women and minorities were treated and worked hard to improve their conditions. She dreamed of a world that was fair and equal for everyone.

GETTING THERE

Roosevelt was a teenager when her parents died. She was raised by her grandmother. A naturally shy person, Roosevelt learned to like the public life after she became the First Lady. Gradually, she realized her gift for public speaking.

? Roosevelt overcame shyness and limited self-confidence to become a great leader. In your own life, what do you strive to overcome to be the best you can be?

Through her speeches and writing, she actively campaigned to recruit female workers to the factories during World War II, while all the men were fighting overseas. With her help, the government funded the building of child-care centers so that mothers could work. During a Southern Conference for Human Welfare in Alabama in 1938, Roosevelt refused to sit in the white section, apart from her black friends. She publicly resigned from the Daughters of the American Revolution because of their racist policies.

HER LEGACY

Roosevelt had humanitarian dreams. She wanted to bring equality to all people in the world, and she did this through her greatest legacy, the Universal Declaration of Human Rights. She also traveled extensively to developing and poor countries, hoping to bring more awareness to the American people of the poverty that exists in the world. She was active in the Red Cross and volunteered her time in Navy hospitals.

Quick Fact

As the First Lady, Roosevelt held press conferences allowing only female journalists. Her reasoning was that if newspapers wanted to be represented at her conferences, then they would have to hire female reporters.

Eleanor Roosevelt sitting on the White House lawn with a group of soldiers during a party in their honor

The Expert Says...

" What other single human being has touched and transformed the existence of so many? She walked in the slums … as one who could not feel contentment when others were hungry. "

— Adlai Stevenson, Ambassador to the United Nations, 1961–1965

10 9 8 7 6

"WHAT THEY SAID"

Eleanor Roosevelt was a great woman who had an impact on the lives of millions. There are many who have been, and who still are, inspired by her, including poets, presidents, and teachers, as you'll read in the quotes below.

"Eleanor Roosevelt is a constant reminder of how much one life can accomplish. Because of her life, millions of people experienced a new sense of possibility."
— **William H. Chafe, Professor of History, Duke University**

"If democracy had saints — and no other cause demands a greater selflessness, a greater devotion — Mrs. Roosevelt would be one. She proved her faith in action as saints do."
— **Archibald MacLeish, poet**

"Her memory and spirit will long endure among those who labor for great causes around the world."
— **John F. Kennedy, former president of the United States**

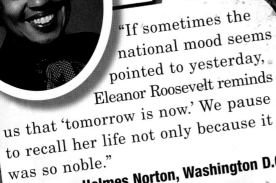

"If sometimes the national mood seems pointed to yesterday, Eleanor Roosevelt reminds us that 'tomorrow is now.' We pause to recall her life not only because it was so noble."
— **Eleanor Holmes Norton, Washington D.C. Delegate to Congress**

Eleanor Roosevelt and John F. Kennedy

"Eleanor Roosevelt understood that every one of us every day has choices to make about the kind of person we are and what we wish to become. ... You have a choice."
— **Hillary Rodham Clinton, former First Lady, now Senator of New York**

"Eleanor possesses a spirit of steel and a heart of gold."
— **Winston Churchill, former prime minister of Britain**

Take Note

Eleanor Roosevelt's legacy puts her on the top of this list of amazing women. All of her work was focused on protecting the rights of children, women, and the disadvantaged. As President Truman once said, she was the "First Lady of the World."

• Research Eleanor Roosevelt and her accomplishments. What do you think was her greatest accomplishment? Why?

We Thought ...

Here are the criteria we used in ranking the 10 most outstanding American women.

This woman:
- Had dedication and desire
- Touched the lives of millions
- Overcame physical challenges and discrimination
- Broke social barriers
- Contributed to literature and the arts
- Greatly influenced the world's views on the environment
- Fought for social justice in the workforce
- Advocated for the rights of women, children, and minorities

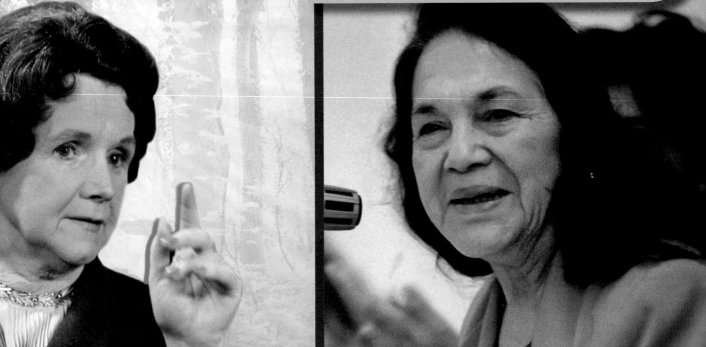

What Do You Think?

1. Do you agree with our ranking? If you don't, try ranking these women yourself. Justify your ranking with data from your own research and reasoning. You may refer to our criteria, or you may want to draw up your own list of criteria.

2. Here are three other outstanding American women we considered but in the end did not include in our top 10 list: Coretta Scott King, Hillary Clinton, and Susan B. Anthony.
   • Find out more about them. Do you think they should have made our list? Give reasons for your response.
   • Are there other outstanding American women who you think should have made our list? Explain your choices.

Index